Piano • Vocal • Guitar

Gospel Songs
Hank Williams

ISBN 978-0-634-00698-2

HAL•LEONARD®
CORPORATION

7777 W. BLUEMOUND RD. P.O. BOX 13819 MILWAUKEE, WI 53213

Visit Hal Leonard Online at
www.halleonard.com

CONTENTS

4	Angel of Death
6	Are You Walkin' and A-Talkin' for the Lord
12	Dear Brother
9	Help Me Understand
14	A Home in Heaven
16	House of Gold
18	How Can You Refuse Him Now
20	I Saw the Light
26	Jesus Died for Me
28	Jesus Is Calling
30	Jesus Remembered Me
32	Last Night I Dreamed of Heaven
34	Message to My Mother
36	Mother Is Gone
38	(I'm Praying for the Day That) Peace Will Come
23	Ready to Go Home
40	We're Getting Closer to the Grave Each Day
42	Wealth Won't Save Your Soul
44	When God Comes and Gathers His Jewels
46	When the Book of Life Is Read

ANGEL OF DEATH

Words and Music by
HANK WILLIAMS

5

ARE YOU WALKIN' AND A-TALKIN' FOR THE LORD

Words and Music by
HANK WILLIAMS

Lord? _____ Would you stop and try to save on your
Lord? _____ Would you stop and shout His name or _____
Lord? _____ Will He stop take you by the hand and lead you

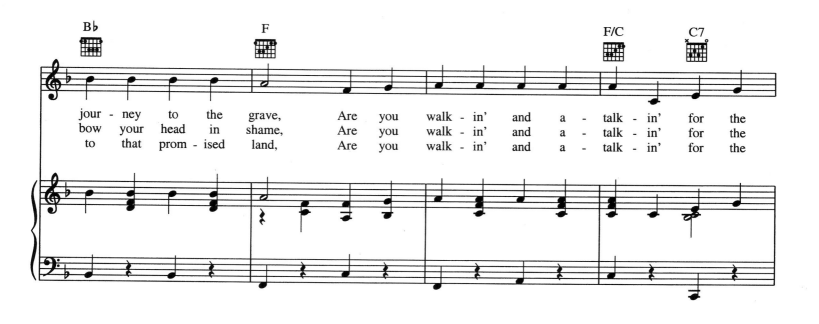

jour - ney to the grave, Are you walk - in' and a - talk - in' for the
bow your head in shame, Are you walk - in' and a - talk - in' for the
to that prom - ised land, Are you walk - in' and a - talk - in' for the

Lord? _____
Lord? _____
Lord? _____

Are you walk - in', (are you walk - in',) Are you

HELP ME UNDERSTAND

Words and Music by
HANK WILLIAMS

Quietly

A lit-tle girl prayed at the close of the

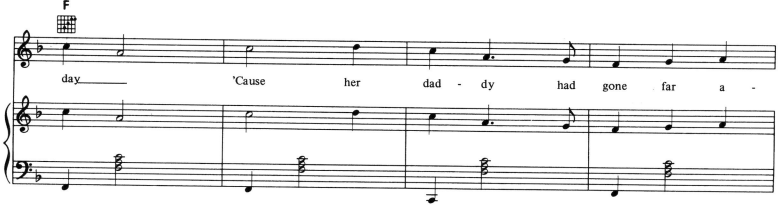

day ___ 'Cause her dad-dy had gone far a-

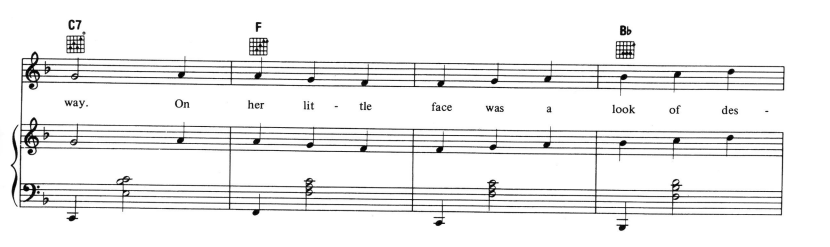

way. On her lit-tle face was a look of des-

take me and lead me and hold to my

hand _____ Oh, Heav - en - ly Fath - er, Help

Me Un - der - stand. Me Un - der - stand.

rit.

RECITATION

You know, Friends, I wonder how many homes are broken tonight - just how many tears are shed.
    By some little word of anger that never should have been said
I'd like to tell you a story of a family I once knew
    We'll call them Mary and William and their little daughter, Sue
Mary was just a plain Mother, and Bill - well, he was the usual Dad
    And they had their family quarrels, like everyone else - but neither one got mad
Then one day something happened - it was nothing, of course
    But one word led to another, and the last word led to a divorce.
Now here were two grown up people who failed to see common sense
    They strengthened their own selfish pride - at little Sue's expense
You know, she didn't ask to be brought into this world - to drift from pillar to post
    But a divorce never stops to consider the one it hurts the most
There'd be a lot more honest lovin' in this wicked world today
    If just a few parted parents could hear little Sue say:

(Repeat Chorus)

DEAR BROTHER

Words and Music by
HANK WILLIAMS

CHORUS

A HOME IN HEAVEN

Words and Music by
HANK WILLIAMS

HOUSE OF GOLD

Words and Music by
HANK WILLIAMS

HOW CAN YOU REFUSE HIM NOW

Words and Music by
HANK WILLIAMS

I SAW THE LIGHT

Words and Music by
HANK WILLIAMS

READY TO GO HOME

Words and Music by
HANK WILLIAMS

JESUS DIED FOR ME

Words and Music by
HANK WILLIAMS

CHORUS

JESUS IS CALLING

Words and Music by HANK WILLIAMS
and CHARLIE MONROE

JESUS REMEMBERED ME

Words and Music by
HANK WILLIAMS

31

LAST NIGHT I DREAMED OF HEAVEN

Words and Music by
HANK WILLIAMS

2nd Chorus

LAST NIGHT I DREAMED OF HEAVEN
That land so pure and sweet
And the joy within me
Made my glad heart weep
I was there with my Saviour
Free from grief and strife
LAST NIGHT I DREAMED OF HEAVEN
The land of eternal life

MESSAGE TO MY MOTHER

Words and Music by
HANK WILLIAMS

CHORUS

Take this MES - SAGE TO MY MOTH - ER

It will fill her heart with joy

Tell her that I've met my Sav - iour God has

saved her wan - d'ring boy. [1.] boy. [2.]

3

Years have passed since that parting
But I know she waits and prays
Soon I'll cross that dark river
Please let her know that I was saved

MOTHER IS GONE

Words and Music by
HANK WILLIAMS

My friends did say before she went away
She called my name o'er and o'er
So trusting in God's love, I'll meet her above
Over on that other shore

(I'm Praying for the Day That)
PEACE WILL COME

Words and Music by HANK WILLIAMS
and PEE WEE KING

WE'RE GETTING CLOSER TO THE GRAVE EACH DAY

Words and Music by
HANK WILLIAMS

On the great judgement day when life's book is read
There'll be no time to pray
Learn to love and forgive while on earth you live
WE'RE GETTING CLOSER TO THE GRAVE EACH DAY.

WEALTH WON'T SAVE YOUR SOUL

Words and Music by
HANK WILLIAMS

WHEN GOD COMES AND GATHERS HIS JEWELS

Words and Music by
HANK WILLIAMS

WHEN THE BOOK OF LIFE IS READ

Words and Music by
HANK WILLIAMS